Frank B. Converse

The Banjo and how to play it

Frank B. Converse

The Banjo and how to play it

ISBN/EAN: 9783744646895

Printed in Europe, USA, Canada, Australia, Japan

Cover: Foto ©Thomas Meinert / pixelio.de

More available books at **www.hansebooks.com**

THE BANJO

AND HOW TO PLAY

BY FRANK B. CONVERSE

NEW YORK

DICK & FITZGERALD, PUBLISHERS.

The Magician's Own Book.

One of the most extraordinary and interesting volumes ever printed—containing the Whole Art of Conjuring, and all the Discoveries in Magic ever made, either by ancient or modern philosophers. IT EXPLAINS

All Sleight of Hand Tricks;
Tricks and Deceptions with Cards;
The Magic of Chemistry;
Mysterious Experiments in Electricity and Galvanism;
The Magic of Pneumatics, Aerostatics, Optics. etc.;
The Magic of Numbers;

Curious Tricks in Geometry;
Mysterious and Amusing Puzzles, and answers thereto;
The Magic of Art;
Miscellaneous Tricks and Experiments;
Curious Fancies, etc., etc.

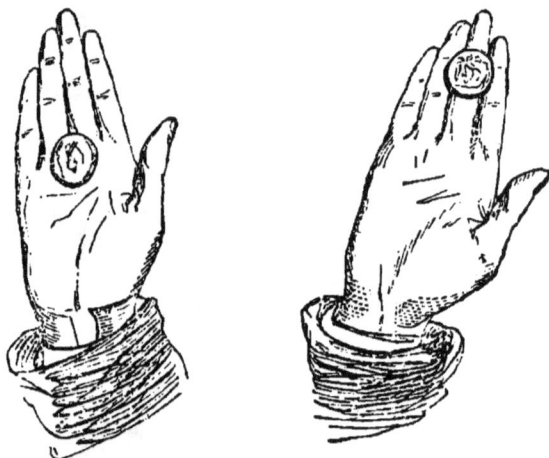

The tricks are all illustrated by Engravings and Tables, so as to make them easily understood and practiced. As a volume for the amusement of an evening party, this book cannot be surpassed. Gilt binding, 362 pages.......................$1.50

East Lynne; or, The Earl's Daughter.

Library edition, complete and unabridged. This novel is Mrs. Henry Wood's masterpiece, and stands in the very front rank of all the works of fiction ever written; it has scarcely a rival as a brilliant creation of literary genius, and is prominent among the very few works of its class that have stood the test of time, and achieved a lasting reputation. In originality of design, and masterly and dramatic development of the subject, East Lynne stands unrivaled; it will be read and re-read long after the majority of the ephemeral romances of to-day have passed out of existence and been forgotten. A handsome 12mo volume of 598 pages, from new electrotype plates, printed on fine toned paper, and elegantly bound in cloth, in black and gold...$1.50

THE BANJO,

AND

HOW TO PLAY IT.

CONTAINING,

IN ADDITION TO THE ELEMENTARY STUDY,

A CHOICE COLLECTION OF POLKAS, WALTZES, SOLOS, SCHOTTISCHES,
SONGS, REELS, HORNPIPES, JIGS, ETC., WITH FULL EXPLANA-
TIONS OF BOTH THE "BANJO" AND "GUITAR" STYLES
OF EXECUTION, AND DESIGNED TO IMPART A
COMPLETE KNOWLEDGE OF THE ART OF
PLAYING THE BANJO PRACTICAL-
LY WITHOUT THE AID
OF A TEACHER.

BY

FRANK B. CONVERSE.

NEW YORK:
DICK & FITZGERALD, PUBLISHERS,
No. 18 ANN STREET.

Electrotyped by SMITH & McDOUGAL, 82 Beckman St.

PREFACE.

In presenting "The Banjo, and How to Play it," to the learners and lovers of the Banjo generally, the author begs he may, without presumption, be allowed to congratulate himself upon the flattering success attained by his former work—"The Banjo without a Master," and in having contributed, in no slight degree, towards abridging and simplifying the study of the Banjo, and thereby removing the many obstacles from the pathway of those who—from want of a competent teacher, or a comprehensible instruction book—have been unable to obtain a mastery over this delightful instrument.

Many of those who essay the Banjo, labor under the impression that to learn and apply correct musical principles to this instrument would be a needless waste of time, and—having heard many persons who execute passably well entirely by ear—quite useless. But this is a great mistake, and none but a person entirely ignorant of the science of music would entertain such an opinion.

Music—like the other sciences—to be understood, requires to be learned systematically; and the elementary principles must be well fixed in the mind before a satisfactory or rapid progress can be expected.

When once the rudiments and the elementary exerciscs are well understood (which amounts to nearly all the study the character of this work requires), each succeeding step becomes comparatively easy, and the more interesting; and the fact that the pupil is performing understandingly gives him an assurance and certainty which this knowledge alone can convey.

The present work is designed to enlarge the learner's knowledge of the instrument, particularly in the Guitar Style of execution—playing accompaniments, Polkas, Waltzes, &c. It also embraces a large collection of Jigs, Hornpipes, &c., to be executed in the regular Banjo style, the whole forming a collection valuable as well to the professional as to the amateur.

With these few remarks I send this little volume forth, sincerely trusting it may receive a share of the favor so generously extended to its companion, "The Banjo without a Master."

THE AUTHOR.

CONTENTS.

THE BANJO,

AND

HOW TO PLAY IT.

RUDIMENTS OF MUSIC.

MUSICAL TONES, or SOUNDS, are represented by characters called notes.

NOTES denote the LENGTH (duration of time) of tones.

RESTS are marks for silence, corresponding in length (duration of time) with the different notes after which they are called.

Notes and Rests.

THE WHOLE NOTE is represented by a character somewhat resembling an italic o, and is the longest note used. As it is usual to measure the length (duration) of tones by counting the whole note has four counts.

THE HALF NOTE is distinguished from the whole note by its having a stem, thus, ♩ or ♩, and has two counts.

THE QUARTER NOTE is represented thus ♩ or ♩; is one-fourth the length—in duration of time—of the whole note, and has one count.

THE EIGHTH NOTE differs from the quarter note in having a hook attached to the stem, thus: ♪ or ♪, and is one half the length of the quarter note, or one eighth the length of the whole note.

THE SIXTEENTH NOTE differs from the eighth in having *two hooks* attached to its stem, thus: ♬ or ♬.

THE THIRTY-SECOND NOTE has three hooks, thus: ♬ or ♬.

Table of Notes and Rests.

Whole Note.	Half Note.	Quarter Note.

Whole Rest.	Half Rest.	Quarter Rest.

Eighth Note.	Sixteenth Note.	Thirty-second Note.

Eighth Rest.	Sixteenth Rest.	Thirty-second Rest.

Dotted Notes and Rests.

A dot placed to the right of, and immediately following a note or rest, adds to the note or rest one half of its original length in duration of time; thus:

A dotted whole note, _o_ . is equal to three half notes.

A dotted half note, _ƒ_ . is equal to three quarter notes.

A dotted quarter note, _ƒ_ . is equal to three eighth notes.

A dotted eighth note, _ƒ_ . is equal to three sixteenth notes.

A dotted sixteenth note, _ƒ_ . is equal to three thirty-second notes.

The Musical Alphabet.

The first seven letters of the Alphabet are used for naming the different tones. As there are a greater number of tones than seven, the letters are repeated as often as may be necessary, thus: A, B, C, D, E, F, G, A, B, C, D, E, F G, A, &c.

The Staff, or Stave.

The staff is composed of five parallel lines and the four intermediate spaces, which, taken collectively, form nine degrees. The names of the notes are determined by the position they occupy upon the staff.

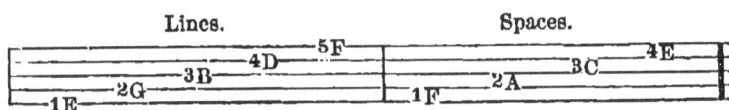

Added, or Leger Lines.

When it is required to extend the scale beyond the limits of the regular staff, then ADDED or LEGER lines are used, and the notes upon these lines are reckoned in the same manner as those upon the staff.

Names of the Notes on the Staff, Leger Lines and Spaces.

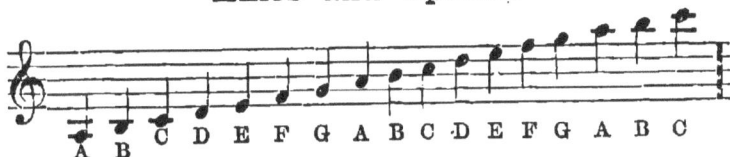

The G, or Treble Clef.

THE TREBLE CLEF is the only one used for banjo music. It resembles, somewhat, a written capital letter S reversed, and is always placed at the beginning of the staff.

G, or Treble Clef.

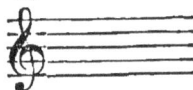

Measures, Bars, Time.

The perpendicular lines drawn across the staff at regular distances are called BARS. The spaces between the bars are called MEASURES. Each measure contains the quantity indicated by the figures placed at the beginning of the piece.

There are three kinds of time, viz: COMMON, TRIPLE, and COMPOUND. In COMMON TIME there are an equal number of parts in a measure; in TRIPLE TIME, three parts; and in COMPOUND TIME, six or more. COMMON TIME has three varieties, viz: $\frac{4}{4}$ (sometimes indicated by the letter C placed at the beginning of the piece) which signifies that each measure contains the value of a whole note. This variety has four beats or counts in each measure. The *second variety* has two beats in each measure and is designated thus: $\frac{2}{4}$. The *third variety* has two beats in each measure, and is designated thus: $\frac{4}{8}$.

Three Varieties of Triple Time

Four Varieties of Compound Time.

The figures signify that each measure contains that portion of a whole note which they fractionally represent of a whole. And, in counting time, the upper figure denotes the number of counts, or beats, in each measure; the lower figure, the value of each count or beat.

The Double Bar.

The double bar is placed at the end of a strain, or at the close of a piece, to denote that a part or the whole is finished.

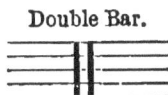

Double Bar.

The Dotted Double Bar.

Dots placed to the right or left of a double bar, denote that the part of the tune on the same side with the dots is to be repeated.

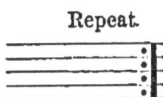

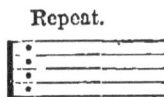

Repeat.   Repeat.

Tones and Semitones.

A SEMITONE is the smallest interval or degree between two musical sounds. If the banjo is correctly fretted, the distance from one fret to the next is a semitone.

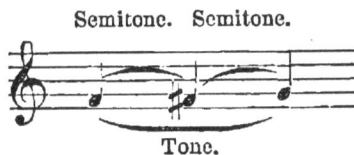

Semitone. Semitone.

Tone.

Sharp, Flat, and Natural.

A SHARP (♯) placed immediately before a note, raises it one semitone, (one fret towards the bridge).

A FLAT (♭) placed before a note lowers it one semitone.

A NATURAL (♮) placed before a note, previously affected by either a *sharp* or *flat*, restores it to its original sound.

The Signature.

The sharps or flats placed at the beginning of a piece form the Signature, thus determining *the key* in which the piece stands. They affect the pitch of the notes throughout the piece bearing the same name.

Accidental Sharp, Flat, or Natural.

When a sharp or flat—not of the signature—is temporarily introduced in the course of a piece, it is termed an *accidental*, and its influence continues only throughout the measure in which it is placed, unless it should be the last note in the measure, and the first note of the following measure begins with the same note, in which case its influence would continue throughout the second measure also. In either case, however, the introduction of an *opposite accidental* would contradict the previous one.

Triplets and Sextoles.

A triplet is composed of three notes, having a curved line and a figure 3 placed either over or under them, thus :

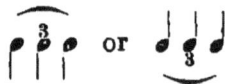

They must be played in the time of two notes of the same denomination.

A sextole is a group embracing six notes having a curved line and the figure 6 placed either over or under. The notes must be played in the time of four notes of the same denomination.

Grace Notes.

Grace notes are small notes introduced to embellish the piece. They make no part of the measure, but partake of the notes before or after which they are placed, and are to be executed in such a manner as not to affect the regularity of the movement.

Chords.

When three or more notes are played together as one, they form a chord. A chord is of the same value in duration of time as a single note of the same denomination.

The Barre.

The barré is made by pressing the first finger of the left hand squarely across the finger-board.

Positions.

Positions are taken at each fret on the finger-board, either with the ordinary fingering or by the barré. When required to be taken they will be denoted by a letter P, placed over the note or chord.

The Pause.

The pause (⌒) is a sign placed over a note or chord to denote that its duration of time may be increased according to the judgment of the performer.

The Tie and Slur.

The TIE is a curved line placed over or under two or more notes occupying the same position upon the staff, and signifies that the first only is to be sounded, and the time of the others counted.

The SLUR is also a curved line, similar to the *tie*, placed over two or more notes, and denotes that the first note only is to be played by the *right hand;* the following notes being produced by quickly and forcibly stopping the strings with the fingers of the left hand.

The Tie.

The Slur.

Diagram of the Finger-board.

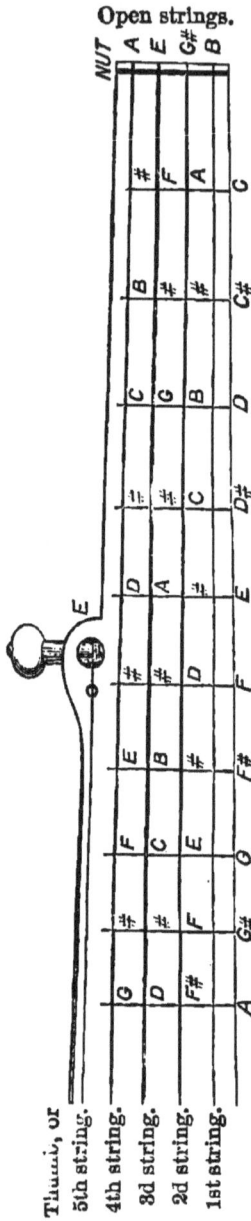

Open strings.

The Regular Scale of the Banjo.

The natural scale of the Banjo requires the aid of three *sharped* notes, viz: the F♯s, C♯s, and G♯s,—establishing the Key of A, (three sharps.) The learner will more readily comprehend this remark by trying the scale on his instrument while referring to the diagram.

Directions for Stringing the Banjo.*

1st String..............a Violin E String.

2d   "   ...."   "   A   "

3d   "   ...."   "   D   "

4th   "   ...." Banjo 4th   "

5th   "   ...." Violin E   "

For the 2d, 3d, and 5th strings, select the lightest of the three varieties.

Tuning.

NOTE.—All banjos do not sound equally well when tuned to the Key of A, in consequence of their varying in length, &c.; but the rule here given, being designed expressly for beginners, will enable them to tune their instruments properly, and, after they have acquired facility in tuning, it will be an easy matter for them to ascertain which key will produce the best quality of tone from the instrument.

An A tuning-fork or pitch-pipe is of great assistance to beginners in learning to tune the banjo. They can be procured from any music dealer.

4TH STRING.

Commence with this string, which tune to A (tuning-fork or pitch-pipe).

3D STRING.

Measure the distance from the nut to the bridge, and at one third of the distance (measuring from the nut) stop the 4th string with the second finger of the left hand, making E. Tune the 3d string in unison with it.

2D STRING.

At one-fifth of the distance, measuring as before, stop the 3d string, making G ♯. Tune the second string in unison with it.

* "Directions for Stringing the Banjo," "Tuning," "Holding the Banjo," and "Signs for Fingering," taken from "FRANK CONVERSE'S Banjo without a Master," No. 1, published by DICK & FITZGERALD.

1st String.

At one third the distance, measuring as before, stop the
3d string with the second finger, making B, tune the 1st
string in unison with it.

Unison.

When two strings are in unison, the sounding one of them,
will cause the other to vibrate.

Test of Tuning.

If the Instrument is in tune, the first three strings,
sounded open, in the following order, thus: 3d, 2d, 1st,
1st, will commence the air of "Oh Susanna." Then by
placing the left hand at the Natural Position (see diagram)
the 4th and 2d strings will sound in unison.

The Banjo in Tune will sound the following Notes.

4th String.	3d String.	2d String.	1st String.	5th String.

Holding the Banjo.

Sit erect. The banjo resting on the front of the right
thigh ; the neck elevated and resting in the left hand between the thumb and forefinger. Rest the right forearm
on the rim of the instrument near the tail-piece. bringing
the wrist over the bridge.

Position of the Right Hand.

Partly close the right hand, allowing the first finger to
project a little in advance of the others. Slightly curve
the thumb. Strike the strings with the first finger (nail)
and pull with the thumb.

Signs for Fingering.

LEFT HAND.

The left hand fingering is written above the notes, thus: 1, 2, 3, 4; the figures naming the fingers required for "stopping" the strings to make the required notes, a small o placed over a note, denotes that the note, over which it is formed, is to be sounded on an open string, that is—*not stopped*. Notes figured thus: 1̲, 2̲, 3̲, 4̲, must be sounded by pulling the string with the finger of the left hand which is numbered in the half circle.

RIGHT HAND.

Right hand fingering is written below the notes, thus: x indicating the thumb, and 1, the first finger. A waved line ⌇, placed under a triplet or any collection of notes, denotes that you must play them by sliding the first finger across the required strings. Notes written thus:

are to be sounded on the fifth (thumb) string by pulling with the thumb.

The Guitar Style of Fingering.

In performing polkas, waltzes, marches, and pieces containing harmony generally, the rule for right-hand fingering heretofore given, having reference solely to what is usually termed the *legitimate banjo style*, does not apply. In the banjo style of execution, melody alone is embraced, or, in other words, the tones follow in succession and are rarely combined. Also the manner of sounding the strings (striking with the nail) produces the quality of tone and other peculiarities characteristic of the genuine banjo music. In the guitar style of execution the manner of sounding the strings is reversed, and, in addition to the thumb and first finger, the remaining fingers are brought into requisition. Instead of striking them with the nail the strings are to be sounded by pulling them with the points of the fingers; and to avoid the clashing sound usually attending the first efforts of beginners, the fingers should meet and draw the strings obliquely, which will cause them to vibrate *across* the finger-board, producing a full and mellow tone. Avoid, from the beginning, the bad habit of supporting the right hand by resting the fourth finger upon the head of the banjo. The forearm resting upon the rim, will do this far better and more gracefully. Besides, the fourth finger is frequently required to be used, and when once the habit of resting it has become fixed, it it will be found an effort of no little difficulty to bring the finger into use when absolutely required.

Signs for Right-Hand Fingering.

GUITAR STYLE.

The signs for the right-hand fingering will be found written either below or placed to the left of the notes upon the staff. The following are the signs:—x, thumb; 1, 1st finger; 2, 2d finger; 3, 3d finger; 4, 4th finger.

The Five Principal Positions.

The "five principal positions" by no means embrace the number that can be taken upon the instrument. On the contrary, positions are taken at every fret upon the finger-board. The five here given are generally the first to be mastered by the learner, and should be thoroughly understood, as they form what might be termed a base of or key to the majority of the positions.

THE FIVE PRINCIPAL POSITIONS.

(See Position, page 7.)

1ST OR NATURAL POSITION.

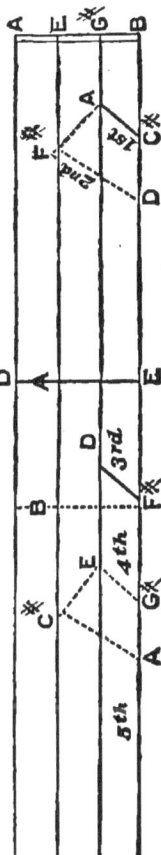

Place the first finger on the 2d string at A, and the second finger on the 1st string at C♯.

2D POSITION.

Place the first finger on the 2d string at A, the second finger on the 3d string at F♯, and the fourth finger on the 1st string at D.

3D POSITION.

Press the first finger across the finger-board at D (on the 4th string) holding down the four strings firmly; then place the third finger on the 2d string, making D, and the fourth finger on the string, making F♯.

4TH POSITION.

Press the first finger across the finger-board at E (on the 4th string); the third and fourth fingers are placed in the same manner as in holding the 3d position, making E and G♯.

5TH POSITION.

Place the first finger on the 2d string at E (of the 4th position), the second finger on the third string at C♯, and the fourth finger on the 1st string at A.

EXERCISES FOR PRACTICE.

A familiarity with the following progressively arranged exercises will materially assist the learner in mastering the regular pieces given in the latter part of this work.

In commencing to learn a new tune, the learner should first ascertain the key in which the piece is written, and also the time or movement in which it is to be performed (see SIG-NATURE), and then—after having carefully read the entire piece, beating and counting aloud the time—commence with the banjo.

No. 1. Banjo Style.

Introducing QUARTER NOTES and QUARTER RESTS.

EXPLANATION.

Natural key of the banjo (3 sharps). Common Time.

Four beats in each measure. A count with each beat. Give to each beat the value* (in duration of time) of one quarter note.

Count 1   2   3   4 or 1 and 2 and 3 and 4 and

1 and 2 and 3 and 4 and

1st Measure.

Hold the natural position. Play 3d string, 2d string, 1st string, 5th string.

2d Measure.

Stop the 1st string with the fourth finger at D (see diagram). Play 1st string. Open strings, play 1st string, 2d string, 3d string.

3d Measure.

Open strings. Play 3d, 2d, 1st, 5th.

4th Measure.

Hold the natural position. Play 1st, 2d, 3d, 4th.

---

* Pronouncing the word "*and*" between the counts completes (in the mind) the duration of time, and thereby assists in regulating the movement.

5TH MEASURE.

Open strings. Play 3d, 1st. Hold the natural position, play 2d.

6TH MEASURE.

Open strings. Play 3d, 5th. Stop the 1st string at D, with the fourth finger, and play 1st. Open strings, play 1st.

7TH MEASURE.

Open strings. Play 3d, 1st, 2d, 5th.

8TH MEASURE.

Hold the natural position. Play 2d (the *Quarter Note*). Give a full beat to the quarter rest. Play the 4th. Give the concluding rest its full beat and count.

No. 2. Banjo Style.

SEE EXPLANATION, No. 1.

1ST MEASURE.

Hold the natural position. Play 1st, 1st, 2d, 3d.

* The " start note " must be counted and played as the finish of a (supposable) preceding full measure.

2D MEASURE.

Open strings.   Play 2d, 1st, 1st, 5th.

3D MEASURE.

Open strings.   Play 1st, 1st, 2d, 3d.

4TH MEASURE.

Hold the natural position. Play 2d, 1st, 1st. Beat upon, and give a full count (4 and) for the Rest.

5TH MEASURE.

Natural position.   Play 5th, 5th, 1st, 2d.

6TH MEASURE.

Hold the 2d position (see " FIVE PRINCIPAL POSITIONS "). Play 3d, 2d, 1st, 3d.

7TH MEASURE.

Natural position.   Play 3d, 5th, 1st, 2d.

8TH MEASURE.

Natural position.   Play 2d, 3d, 4th.   Give the concluding *Rest* its full beat and count.

No. 3. Banjo Style.

Introducing EIGHTH NOTES, and EIGHTH RESTS ; Dotted Eighth notes and eighth rests (see DOTTED NOTES and RESTS), followed by a sixteenth note, and dotted quarter notes.

EXPLANATION.

Natural key of the banjo (3 sharps). Common time. Four beats (with counts) in each measure. The beat equals a quarter note or its equivalent in value of time. The following are the equivalents of a quarter note introduced in this exercise :—

also the dot placed after the quarter note in the sixth measure, taken in connection with the EIGHTH NOTE that follows, equals a quarter note.

1ST MEASURE.

Natural position, play 1st, 1st, 1st. Open strings, play 1st, 2d, 1st, 5th.

2D MEASURE.

Natural position, play 2d, 3d, 4th, 1st, 5th.

3D MEASURE.

Stop D on the 1st string with the fourth finger. Play 1st, 1st, 5th. Take the natural position and play 1st, 2d, 1st, 5th.

4TH MEASURE.

Open strings, play 1st, 5th, 5th. Count upon the "*rest*" and follow with 1st (eighth note), 2d, 1st.

5TH MEASURE.

Natural position, play 1st, 2d. Open strings, play 1st, 5th, 1st, 2d.

6TH MEASURE.

Stop A (at the natural position) on the 2d string with the first finger. Play 2d, 2d, 2d. The next note (G ♯) is to be sounded by pulling the string with the first finger of the left hand—sounding the string open (see LEFT HAND FINGERING). Stop F ♯ on the 3d string (see DIAGRAM) with the second finger, play 3d, 1st.

7TH MEASURE.

Open strings, play 3d. Count on the "*rest*" and allow for the dot, play 3d. Stop F ♯ as before and play 3d, 2d.

8TH MEASURE.

Natural position, play 2d, 3d, 4th.

No. 4. Banjo Style.

NOTE.—In playing the dotted eighth note and the sixteenth note, thus: , care must be taken to properly divide the quantity of time, and give to each its true proportion (see DOTTED NOTES).

SEE EXPLANATION, No. 3.

1st Measure.

Natural position, play 1st, 5th. Retain the natural position, and stop D on the 1st string with the fourth finger, play 1st, 5th. Remove the fourth finger and hold the natural position, play 1st, 5th. Open strings, play 1st, 5th.

2d Measure.

The same as 1st measure.

3d Measure.

Natural position, play 1st, 2d. Retain the natural position and stop D on the 1st string, play 1st, 5th. Remove the fourth finger and hold the natural position, play 1st, 2d. Open strings, play 1st, 2d.

4th Measure.

The same as 3d measure.

5th Measure.

Observe the same changes of fingering as given in the 1st measure, and play 1st, 5th, 1st, 2d, 1st, 5th, 1st, 2d.

6th Measure.

Natural position, play 1st, 5th. Beat upon, and allow the full time for the *dotted eighth rest.* Retain natural position and play 5th, 1st, 5th. Remove the *second finger only,* from the 1st string, continuing to stop the 2d string at A with the first finger, play 2d.

7TH MEASURE.

Observe the same changes of fingering as given in the 5th measure, and play 1st, 2d, 1st, 5th, 1st, 2d, 1st, 5th.

8TH MEASURE.

Natural position, play 1st, 2d. Stop the first string at D with the fourth finger, play 1st, 5th. Open strings, play 1st, 2d. Natural position, play 2d.

No. 5. Banjo Style.

EXPLANATION.

Natural key of the banjo. 2d variety of common time. Two beats (or counts) in each measure. Each beat (or count) has the value of one quarter note, the same as in the 1st variety of common time. Four sixteenth notes equal one quarter note in duration of time, and therefore, they must be played in one count (or beat).

1st Measure.

Natural position, play 1st, 1st. Pull the 1st string open with the second finger of the left hand—sounding B (1st string open). Stop A on the 2d string with the first finger, and, after sounding it, pull it open, which sounds the first note (G ♯) of the 2d measure.

2d Measure.

The first note having been explained in "1st measure," stop F ♯ on the 3d string with the second finger, and play 3d, 3d, 3d.

3d Measure.

Hold the 2d position (see "The Five Principal Positions "). Play 1st, 1st, 3d, 1st.

4th Measure.

Stop F ♯ on the 3d string with the second finger, and sound it; after which, pull the string open with the same finger—sounding E (3d string). Play 3d.

5th Measure.

The same as 1st measure.

6th Measure.

Sound the first note by pulling the 2d string open with the first finger of left hand, which finished the preceding measure by holding A (2d string). Take the 2d position, play 3d, 3d, 5th.

7th Measure.

Open strings, play 3d, 2d, 1st. Natural position, play 1st.

8TH MEASURE.

Sound the first note (B) by pulling the first string open with the second finger of left hand, which finished the preceding measure by holding C ♯ on 1st string. Open strings, play 2d. Natural position, play 2d. The two eighth rests which conclude this measure equal one quarter note in duration of time. (See " DOUBLE BAR.")

9TH MEASURE.

The beginning of the second strain. Natural position, play 3d, 2d, 1st, 5th, 1st, 2d.

10TH MEASURE.

Second position, play 3d, 1st, 3d, 1st.

11TH MEASURE.

Open strings, play 3d, 2d, 1st, 5th, 1st, 2d.

12TH MEASURE.

Natural position, play 2d, 1st, 5th.

13TH MEASURE.

The same as 9th measure.

14TH MEASURE.

Stop D on the 1st string with the fourth finger, play 1st, 1st, and then pull the 1st string open with the fourth finger of left hand—sounding B (1st string), play 5th.

15TH MEASURE.

Open strings, play 3d, 2d, 1st, 5th, 1st, 2d.

16TH MEASURE.

Open strings, play 1st, 2d. Natural position, play 2d.

No. 6. Banjo Style.

EXPLANATION.

Natural key of the banjo. Compound Time. Six eighth notes—or their equivalent—are required to fill a measure. Each eighth note is entitled to one count, therefore there must be six counts in each measure. Beat only on the first and third counts.

PADDY GO DOWN.

1ST MEASURE.

Natural position, play 1st, 2d, 2d. Remove the second finger only from the 1st string. Play 1st, 2d, 2d.

2D MEASURE.

The same as 1st measure.

3D MEASURE.

Position, stop F ♯ on the 3d string with the second finger; and A on the 2d string with the first finger, play 3d, 1st, 1st, 1st, 2d, 1st.

4TH MEASURE.

The same as 3d measure.

5TH MEASURE.

The same as 1st measure.

6TH MEASURE.

The same as 1st measure.

7TH MEASURE.

Stop A on the 2d string with the first finger, play 4th, 2d, 2d, 2d. Pull the 2d string open with the first finger of left hand, sounding G ♯ (2d string). Immediately replace the first finger at A, and sound it.

8TH MEASURE.

Stop A on the 2d string with the first finger, play 4th, 2d, 2d, 2d.

9TH MEASURE.

Natural position, play 1st. Stop D on 1st string with the fourth finger, play 1st, 5th. Open strings, play 1st. Natural position, play 1st. Again stop D on the 1st string as before, and sound it.

10th Measure.

Natural position, play 1st. After which pull the 1st string open with the second finger of the left hand, sounding B (1st string). Natural position, play 1st, 2d. Remove the fingers. Stop F♯ on the 3d string with the second finger, sound, and then pull it open with the second finger, making the two notes F♯ and E.

11th Measure.

The same as 3d measure.

12th Measure.

The same as 3d measure.

13th Measure.

The same as 9th measure.

14th Measure.

The same as 10th measure.

15th Measure.

The same as 7th measure.

16th Measure.

The same as 8th measure.

No. 7. Guitar Style.

See "Guitar Style of Fingering."

EXPLANATION.

Natural key of the banjo. Triple Time. Three quarter notes—or their equivalent—are required to fill a measure. Each quarter note (or quarter rest) is entitled to one count, consequently there will be three counts in each measure. Beat only on the first count in each measure.

1st Measure.

Open strings, play 3d. Natural position, play 2d. Open strings, play 1st.

2d Measure.

Natural position, play 1st. Open strings, play 2d.

3d Measure.

Open strings, play 1st. Stop A on the 2d string with the first finger and sound it.

4th Measure.

Open strings, play 2d. Stop F♯ on the 3d string with the second finger and sound it.

5TH MEASURE.

Open strings, play 3d, 1st. Stop D on the 1st string with the fourth finger and sound it.

6TH MEASURE.

Hold the 2d position, play 3d, 1st.

7TH MEASURE.

Open strings, play 2d. Stop D on the 1st string with the fourth finger and sound it.

8TH MEASURE.

Natural position, play 1st, 2d.

9TH MEASURE.

Natural position, play 4th, 2d. Open strings, play 1st.

10TH MEASURE.

Natural position, play 1st. Stop D on the 1st string and play 1st, 5th.

11TH MEASURE.

Stop D on *the 4th string* with the fourth finger (see diagram) play 4th, 1st (while removing the fourth finger). Natural position, play 1st.

12TH MEASURE.

Stop D on the 1st string with the fourth finger, play 1st, 5th. Raise the left hand and shift down the finger-board (towards the bridge) in position to stop F ♯ (see Diagram), sound it.

13TH MEASURE.

Open strings, play 3d, 2d. Stop A on the 2d string with the first finger, and sound it.

14TH MEASURE.

Open strings, play 1st. Stop F♯ on the 3d string with the second finger, play 3d, 2d.

15TH MEASURE.

Natural position, play 2d, 3d, 1st.

16TH MEASURE.

Natural position, play 2d.

No. 8.

Use both the "BANJO" and "GUITAR" styles of fingering, alternately, in practising the three following exercises.

THAT YOUNG GAL FROM NEW JERSEY.

No. 9.

FOLKS THAT PUT ON AIRS.

No. 10.

RATTLESNAKE JIG.

A Triplet is introduced in the 4th measure (see TRIP-LETS).

No. 11.　Guitar Fingering.

ACCOMPANIMENT.

Several notes written with but one stem, form a CHORD, and all the notes so placed must be sounded together—as one note. The chord is of the same value in duration of time as a single note of the same variety.

No. 12. Guitar Fingering.

ACCOMPANIMENT. BROKEN CHORDS.

No. 13. Guitar Fingering

THE ORIOLE WALTZ.

No. 14. Guitar Fingering.

MELROSE POLKA.

By G. F. HARTLEY.

EXPLANATION.

Key of E, which requires *four* sharps to form the signature. The F♯, C♯ and G♯, forming the signature of the "Natural Key of the Banjo," are retained, to which is added D♯, and, therefore, all the D's must be "sharped"—stopped one half tone (one fret) higher than when executing in the "Natural Key." For an explanation of the *accidental sharps, grace notes* and *triplets* occurring in this piece, see "ACCIDENTALS," "GRACE NOTES," and "TRIPLETS." Tune the 4th string to B—an octave below the 1st string.

1st Measure.

Open strings, play 2d, 1st, 3d, 2d, 1st, 3d.

2d Measure.

Stop C♯ on the 1st string (at the natural position) with the second finger; sound it and *immediately* pull the string open with the second finger of the left hand, thus making the grace note (C♯) and the note following it (B, open string). Stop A♯ on the 2d string (2d fret) with the second finger, play 2d, 1st. Again stop C♯, on the 1st string, as before ; sound and pull the string open, not so quickly as in making the grace note, but giving the note its proper length. After which, play 2d, 3d.

3D MEASURE.

In taking the 2d position (see FIVE PRINCIPAL POSI-TIONS), which must be held throughout this measure, remember the D (on 1st string with the fourth finger) must be stopped *sharp*. Play 4th, 3d, 2d, 1st, 1st.

4TH MEASURE.

Open strings, play 3d, 2d, 1st, 5th. Make the grace note and the one following it, as explained in 2d measure. Open strings, play 2d, 3d, 2d.

5TH MEASURE.

The same as the 1st measure.

6TH MEASURE.

The same as the 2d measure.

7TH MEASURE.

The same as the 3d measure.

8TH MEASURE.

Open strings, play 3d, 3d, 2d, 1st, 5th.

9TH MEASURE.

Hold the natural position, play 3d, 2d, 1st (the chord). The three following notes for a *triplet*, (see TRIPLETS). Hold the natural position and play 3d, 2d, 1st, 5th, 2d.

10TH MEASURE.

The same as the 2d measure.

11TH MEASURE.

The same as the 3d measure.

12TH MEASURE.

The same as the 4th measure.

13TH MEASURE.

The same as the 9th measure.

14TH MEASURE.

The same as the 10th measure.

15TH MEASURE.

The same as the 3d measure.

16TH MEASURE.

Open strings, play 3d, 2d, 1st, 5th, 2d, 1st, 5th.

No. 15. Guitar Fingering.

SEE EXPLANATION OF No. 14.

FAIRYLAND WALTZ.

1st Measure.

Open strings, play 3d, 2d, 1st—*grace notes*, 5th. Stop D (sharp) on the 1st string with the fourth finger, play 1st. Natural position, play 5th, 1st, 2d, 1st.

2d Measure.

Open strings, play 2d, 1st, 5th, 3d, 2d, 1st.

3D MEASURE.

Take the "2d Position," *leaving the 1st string open*, play 4th, 3d, 2d, 1st. Stop D♯ on the 1st string, sound and then pull it open, making D♯ and B.

4TH MEASURE.

Open strings, play 3d, 2d, 1st, 5th. Shift down the fingerboard to G♯ (1st string), stop with the fourth finger, sound and pull it open, making G♯ and B (open string).

5TH MEASURE.

The same as the 1st measure.

6TH MEASURE.

The same as the 2d measure.

7TH MEASURE.

The same as the 3d measure.

8TH MEASURE.

Open strings, play the chord 3, 2, 1, 5. Give to the *rest* its proper count and time which concludes the 1st strain (see DOUBLE BAR). Connect the following strain *in time* by counting the two starting notes as the finish or completion of the preceding measure.

9TH MEASURE.

The *grace note* and the two notes following (B and A♯), were explained in the 2d measure of No. 14. Place the first finger on the 2d string at the natural position (holding A), play 2d.

10TH MEASURE.

Take the "2D POSITION," play 4th, 3d, 2d, 1st, 3d, 2d.

11TH MEASURE.

See the 9th measure for explanation of the first three notes. Open strings, play 4th.

12TH MEASURE.

Open strings, play 3d, 2d, 1st, 5th, 2d, 1st.

13TH MEASURE.

Open strings, play 3d. Stop F♯ on the 3d string (2d fret) with the second finger, and sound it. Open strings, play 2d.

14TH MEASURE.

Natural position, play 2d, 3d, 2d, 1st, 5th.

15TH MEASURE.

Take the " 2D POSITION," play 4th, and the chords 3, 2, 1—3, 2, 1.

16TH MEASURE.

Open strings, play the chord 3, 2, 1, 5, concluding the second strain. For commencing the following strain see explanation of 8th measure.

17TH MEASURE.

Open strings, play 4, 1. Stop C♯ (1st string) with the second finger, at the natural position, play 1st. Stop D♯ (1st string) with the fourth finger, play 4, 1.

18TH MEASURE.

Open strings, play the chord 3, 2, 1, 5—3d, 2d, 1st. Repeat the chord 3, 2, 1, 5.

19TH MEASURE.

The same as the 3d measure.

20TH MEASURE.

The same as the 4th measure.

21ST MEASURE.

The same as the 17th measure.

22D MEASURE.

Open strings, play the chord 3, 2, 1, 5—3d, 2d, 1st, 3d, 2d.

23D MEASURE.

The same as the 15th measure.

24TH MEASURE.

The same as the 16th measure.

No. 16. Guitar Fingering.

THE GAZELLE POLKA.

The first strain of this polka is written in the natural key of the banjo (A, three sharps). The second strain is in the key of E, and requires four sharps for the signature. The additional sharp is D, and therefore all the notes bearing that name must be stopped one half tone (one fret) higher than when executing in the "Natural key." For an explanation of accidental sharps, which occur in the 3d and 4th measures, the pupil will see "ACCIDENTALS;" also consult THE DIAGRAM.

3D MEASURE.

Natural position, play 1st, after which pull the 1st string open with the first finger of left hand, sounding B (1st string). Play 1st. A♯ will be found on the 2d string, at the second fret. See DIAGRAM. Stop it with the second finger and play 2d, 1st.

4TH MEASURE.

Hold the natural position. Stop D on the 1st string with the fourth finger, play 1st. Remove the fourth finger *only* and play 1st. Place the first finger *on the first string* between the second finger (which continues to stop C♯ on the first string) and the Nut (at the fret). Play 1st, and then pull the string with the second finger of left hand (holding the first finger firmly down) sounding B♮. Replace

the second finger as before, and play 1st. See " DOTTED
DOUBLE BAR." DA CAPO or D. C. AL FINE is a musical
term which directs the performer to repeat the piece from
the beginning, and finish at the word FINE.

No. 17. Guitar Fingering.

THE GEM WALTZ.

SEE EXPLANATION OF No. 16.

The word " FINE " is a musical term indicating the end
or finish. Da Capo—generally written D. C.—indicates
that the performer must return to and finish with the first
strain. For an explanation of the slurs which are introduced in this piece, see " THE SLUR."

1ST MEASURE.

Natural position, play 5th, 1st, 2d, 3d.

2D MEASURE.

Stop E♯ on the 3d string (1st fret) with the first finger, sound and immediately stop the same string with the second finger at the 2d fret *sounding F♯*—the result of the slur. Play D, and C♯.

3D MEASURE.

Stop C♯ on the 1st string (2d fret) with the second finger, sound and *immediately* after pull the string open, making the *grace* note (C♯) and the following note (B). Stop A♯ on the 2d string at the 2d fret, with the second finger, play 2d. Open strings, play 1st, 3d, 2d, 1st.

4TH MEASURE.

Hold A on the 2d string, with the first finger, at natural position, play 2d, 3d, 2d. With the second finger of *left hand* pull the first string open, sounding B. Natural position, play 1st. Stop D (1st string) with fourth finger and sound it.

5TH MEASURE.

The same as the 1st measure.

6TH MEASURE.

The same as the 2d measure.

7TH MEASURE.

The same as the 3d measure.

8TH MEASURE.

Natural position, play 4, 2.

9TH MEASURE.

The grace note (C♯) and the note following (B) were explained in the 3d measure. Hold A on 2d string at 1st fret, with the first finger, and F♯ on the 3d string with the second finger, play 2d, 3d, 2d, 1st. Stop D on the 1st string, as before, and sound it.

10TH MEASURE.

Open strings, play 5th, 3d, 2d, 1st, 3d, 2d.

11TH MEASURE.

Stop B on the 2d string, at the 2d fret, with the second finger, and sound it. Hold the 2d position, play the chords 3, 2, 1—3, 2, 1.

12TH MEASURE.

Open strings, play 3d, and the chord 3, 2, 1, 5. Natural position, play 1st.

13TH MEASURE.

The same as the 9th measure.

14TH MEASURE.

The same as the 10th measure.

15TH MEASURE.

The same as the 11th measure.

16TH MEASURE.

Open strings, play the chord 3, 2, 1, 5.

No. 18.

KENTUCKY JUBA.

This and the following exercises are designed to portray the peculiar characteristics of the genuine banjo style. To obtain the desired effect, the notes should be played *staccato*, i. e., distinct and detached from each other, and the fingering strictly followed. Use the "Guitar Style" for the chords, and the regular "Banjo Style" (thumb and forefinger nail) in executing the single notes.

EXPLANATION.

Second variety of common time. Two quarter notes or their equivalents fill a measure. The following are equivalents:

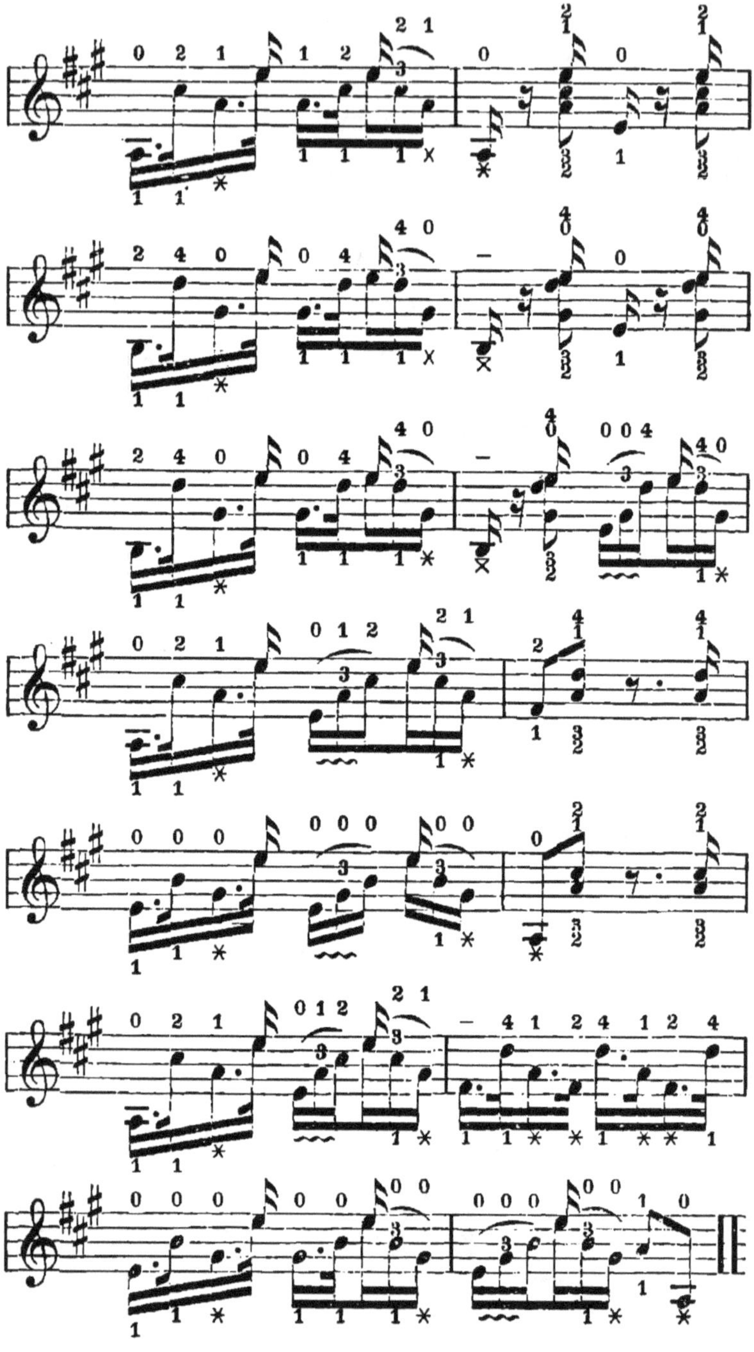

1st Measure.

Natural position, play 4th, 1st, 2d, 5th—2d, 1st, 5th, 1st, 2d.

2d Measure.

Natural position, play 4th, 2, 1, 5, 3d, 2, 1, 5.

3d Measure.

Natural position, play 4th, 1st, 2d, 5th—2d, 1st, 5th, 1st, 2d.

4th Measure.

Natural position, play 4th, 2, 1, 5, 3d, 2, 1, 5.

5th Measure.

Hold B, on the 4th string, with the second finger (see diagram), and D, on the 1st string, with the fourth finger, play 4th, 1st, 2d, 5th—2d, 1st, 5th, 1st, 2d.

6th Measure.

Hold the position described in the 5th measure, play 4th, 2, 1, 5—3d, 2, 1, 5.

7th Measure.

The same as the 5th measure.

8th Measure.

Hold the position described in the 5th measure, play 4th, 2, 1, 5—3, 2, 1, 5, 1, 2.

9th Measure.

Natural position, play 4th, 1st, 2d, 5th—3d, 2d, 1st, 5th, 1st, 2d.

10th Measure.

Hold the 2d position (see " The Five Principal Positions,) play 3d, 2, 1,—2, 1.

11TH MEASURE.

Open strings, play 3d, 1st, 2d, 5th—3d, 2d, 1st, 5th, 1st, 2d.

12TH MEASURE.

Natural position, play 4th, 2, 1—2, 1.

13TH MEASURE.

Natural position, play 4th, 1st, 2d, 5th—3d, 2d, 1st, 5th, 1st, 2d.

14TH MEASURE.

Hold the 2d position (see 10th measure), play 3d, 1st, 2d, 3d—1st, 2d, 3d, 1st.

15TH MEASURE.

Open strings, play 3d, 1st, 2d, 5th—2d, 1st, 5th, 1st, 2d.

16TH MEASURE.

Open strings, play 3d, 2d, 1st, 5th, 1st, 2d. Take the natural position and play 2d, 4th.

No. 19.

GRAPE VINE REEL.

EXPLANATION.

See "GRACE NOTES," and "FINGERING."

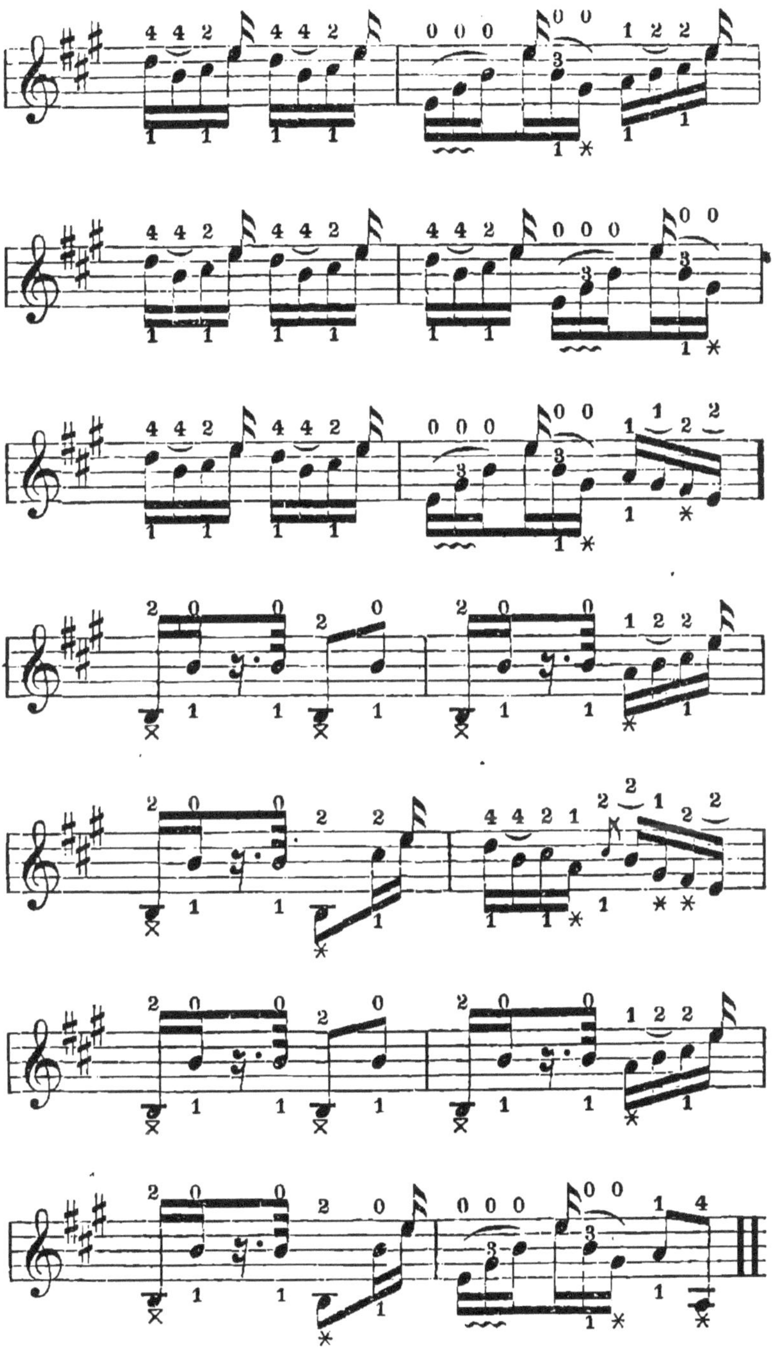

56   THE BANJO,

1st Measure.

Stop D, on the 1st string, with the fourth finger, play 1st, and then pull the 1st string open with the fourth finger, sounding B (1st string open). Natural position, play 1st, 5th. The last four notes are executed in the same manner.

2d Measure.

The first four notes are the same as the first four of the preceding measure. Open strings, play 3d, 2d, 1st, 5th, 1st, 2d.

3d Measure.

The same as the 1st measure.

4th Measure.

Open strings, play 3d, 2d, 1st, 5th, 1st, 2d. Natural position, play 2d, and then with these cond finger of the left hand, pull the first string open, sounding B. Natural position, play 1st, 5th.

5th Measure.

The same as the 1st measure.

6th Measure.

The same as the 2d measure.

7th Measure.

The same as the 1st measure.

8th Measure.

Open strings, play 3d, 2d, 1st, 5th, 1st, 2d. Stop A, on the 2d string, with the first finger (see Diagram) sound, and then pull it open with the finger stopping it making G♯ (2d string open). Stop F♯, on the 3d string, with the second finger of the left hand; sound, and then pull it open with the second finger of the left hand, making E (3d string open).

9TH MEASURE.

Stop B on the 4th string with the second finger, play 4th, 1st, 1st, 4th, 1st.

10TH MEASURE.

Continue to hold B as in the preceding measure, play 4th, 1st, 1st. Natural position, play 2d, and then pull the 1st string open with the second finger of the left hand. Natural position, play 1st, 5th.

11TH MEASURE.

Hold B on the 4th string, play 4th, 1st, 1st, 4th. Natural position, play 1st, 5th.

12TH MEASURE.

Stop D on the 1st string with the fourth finger, sound and then pull it open, making D, and B. Natural position, play 1st, 2d (see GRACE NOTES). Stop C♯ on the 1st string (see DIAGRAM) with the second finger, sound and pull nearly simultaneously, thus making the grace note and the one following (B). Place the first finger on the second string at A, and the second finger on the 3d string at F♯. Play 2d, 3d, and then pull the 3d string open with the second finger of the left hand making E (3d string open).

13TH MEASURE.

The same as the 9th measure.

14TH MEASURE.

The same as the 10th measure.

15TH MEASURE.

Hold B, on the 4th string, play 4th, 1st, 1st, 4th, 1st, 5th.

16TH MEASURE.

Open strings, play 3d, 2d, 1st, 5th, 1st, 2d. Natural position, play 2d, 4th.

MISCELLANEOUS.

ROCKY ROAD TO DUBLIN. *Irish Jig.*

EXPLANATION.

In this piece the C's and G's must be played *natural* [one semitone (one fret) lower than when executing in the " Natural Key " of the banjo] except where they are controlled by an *accidental* sharp. Pay particular attention to the *slurs*, as they naturally assist in the execution.

SPRIG OF SHILLALAH. *Irish Jig.*

THE KILKENNY LADS. *Irish Jig.*

(SEE EXPLANATION ROCKY ROAD TO DUBLIN.)

THE WRECKER'S CLOG HORNPIPE.

ROYAL CLOG HORNPIPE.

THE SILVER HEEL. *Jig.*

SPREAD EAGLE. Reel.

THE GLEN WALTZ.

G. H. BISBEE.

THE ADA WALTZ.

CHAS. HARRIS.

THE PET POLKA.

CHAS. HARRIS.

THE CLARA POLKA.

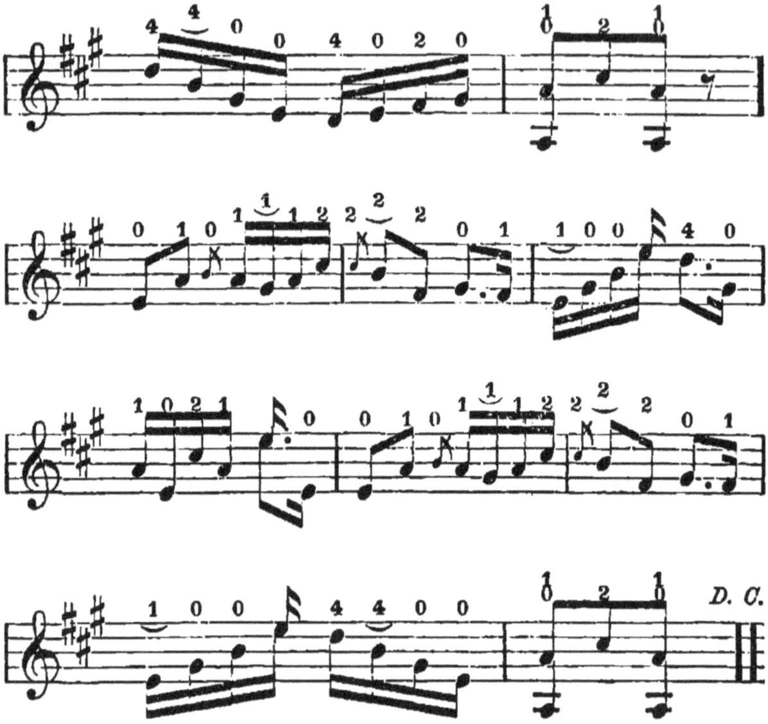

MIGNONETTE SCHOTTISCHE.

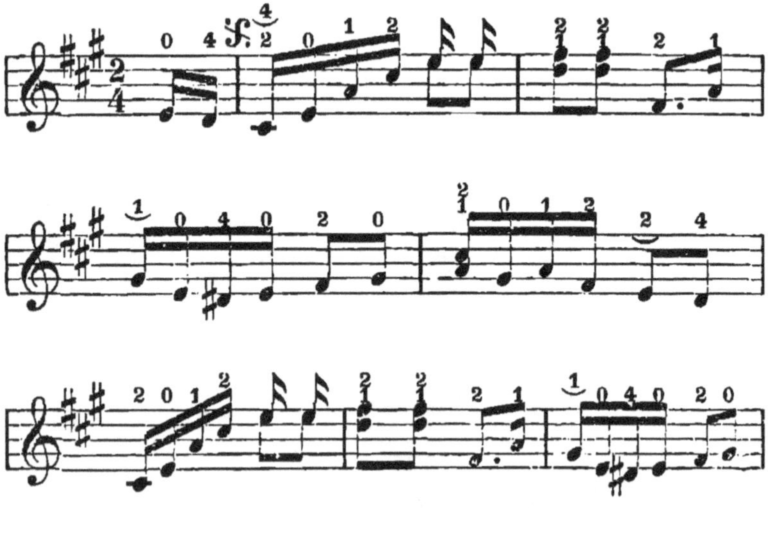

IF EVER I CEASE TO LOVE.

Prelude.

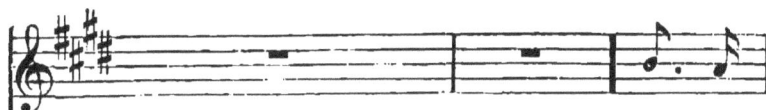

1. In a

house, in   a square, in   a   quadrant,   In a
Turn to   the left   on   the   right hand,   You

street, in   a lane, in   a   road,.....
see   there my true love's a - bode;.....

I   go there a - courting and cooing, To my love like a

dove,   And swearing on   my bend- ed knee If

ev-er I cease to love; May sheepsheads grow on

ap - ple trees, If ev-er I cease to love....

Chorus.

If ev - er I cease to love, ... If

ev-er I cease to love, May the moon be turn'd in-

to green cheese, If ev- er I cease to love.

2 She can sing, she can play the piano,
     She can jump, she can dance, she can run,
  In fact she's a modern Taglioni
  And Sims Reeves rolled into one.
  And who would not love such a beauty,
     Like an angel dropped from above,
  May I be stung to death with flies,
     If ever I cease to love ;
  May I be stung to death with flies,
     If ever I cease to love.

          If ever I cease to love,
          If ever I cease to love,
          May little dogs wag their tails in front,
          If ever I cease to love.

3 For all the money that's in the bank,
     For the title of a lord or a duke,
  I wouldn't exchange the girl I love,
     There's bliss in every look ;
  To see her dance the polka
     I could faint with radiant love,
  May the Monument a hornpipe dance
     If ever I cease to love ;
  May we never have to pay the income tax
     If ever I cease to love.

          If ever I cease to love,
          If ever I cease to love,
          May we all turn into cats and dogs,
          If ever I cease to love.

IT'S NAUGHTY, BUT IT'S NICE.

Written and Composed by ARTHUR LLOYD.

Grove ; At the charming game of cro-quet, I have

been her part-ner twice,   I   love her, ain't   it

naughty ; Well it's naughty, but it's   nice.

Chorus.

You   can-not   say   it's   wick-ed, For   it's

not a glar-ing vice, You can ou-ly say it's

naughty; Well, it's naughty but it's nice.

2 Last night I called at Dudley's Grove,
   And asked if she would go
A walk, and we would talk of love ;
   At first she answered, "No,"
Then consented, and we walked and talked,
   I thought it Paradise ;
But she said 'twas wrong ; I answered,
   Well, it's naughty, but it's nice.—Cho.

3 I put my arm around her waist,
   Her form I gently pressed ;
And then she laid her lovely face
   Upon my manly chest.
I kissed her two times on the cheek,
   I would have kissed her thrice;
But I whispered, Ain't it naughty ?
   She said, Yes, but it's so nice.—Cho.

4 To-day she asked if she might wed:
   Her ma exclaimed, My dear !

You must not think of marrying Fred
For many and many a year.
It's wicked, miss, your pa and ma
And home to sacrifice;
To get married: well, I know, said she,
It's naughty, but it's nice.
Cho.—If you think marriage wicked, ma,
You're guilty of that vice;
You, perhaps, may call it naughty,
But you also know it's nice.

5 Her parents have consented, and
In two years she will be
My wife; so now you know my tale,
I hope you will give to me
The same applause that from you all
So often I entice;
It's naughty, perhaps, to ask it,
But to get it is so nice.—Cho.

THE FASCINATING SWELL.

Words by DICK WEAVER.   Music by FRANK VAN HESS.

1. Oh!
2. If

here I am a - gain, my boys, Just take a look at
on Broadway I chance to go, To take a lit - tle

me :   A nob - by fas - ci - nat - ing swell, So
walk,   The la - dies all stare at me so, And

jol - ly and so free.   The pet of all the
then commence to talk.   They smile and say, "Oh,

girls am I, As an - y one can tell,   In -
ain't he sweet ?" And then each charming belle   Will

deed they've all gone cra - zy o'er This fas - ci - nat - ing
heave a sigh as she passes by This fas - ci - nat - ing

Chorus.

swell.   For they can't   re - sist   my
swell.

fig - ure, boys,   It's the style that

suits   so   well,........   The girls are

grow - ing cra - zy o'er This

fas - ci - nat - ing swell.........

3 At all the balls and parties
    I am always to be found,
For where the girls do congregate,
    You'll find me, I'll be bound.
And there I trip the light fantastic
    With some charming belle,
Who talks sweet loving nonsense to
    This fascinating swell.
        Cho.—For they can't resist, &c.

4 But soon a married man I'll be,
    For t'other day as I
Was walking out I chanced to see
    A pretty girl go by.
She winked at me, I winked at her,
    Then straight in love she fell
With Charles Augustus Fitz de Gray,
    The fascinating swell.
        Cho.—For they can't resist, &c,

UPON THE DANUBE RIVER.

Words by GEORGE COOPER.

Prelude.

1. We glid - ed o'er the rip - pling wave, That
in the star-light dances, To lov - ing looks you
fond - ly gave, The bright - est, sweet - est

glances. We watch'd the sil - ver rays of night A -

bove us soft - ly quiver: Oh ! life was fair and

ro - sy bright, Up - on the Dan - ube riv-er.

Chorus.

We watch'd the sil - ver rays of light A -

bove us soft - ly quiver; Oh! life was fair, and

ro - sy bright, Up - on the Dan - ube riv - er!

2 I held your little hand in mine,
And thought not of the morrow!
I saw your eyes in beauty shine,
Undimmed by clouds of sorrow.
I would that both our lives might flow
As calmly on forever;
'Twas Cupid at the helm, you know,
Upon the Danube river!

Cho.—We watched the silver rays, &c.

MERRY BELLS WALTZ.

THE ZEPHYR WALTZ.

THE DAWN WALTZ.

JIM GILWAY'S FAVORITE HORNPIPE.

MAAS' FAVORITE HORNPIPE.

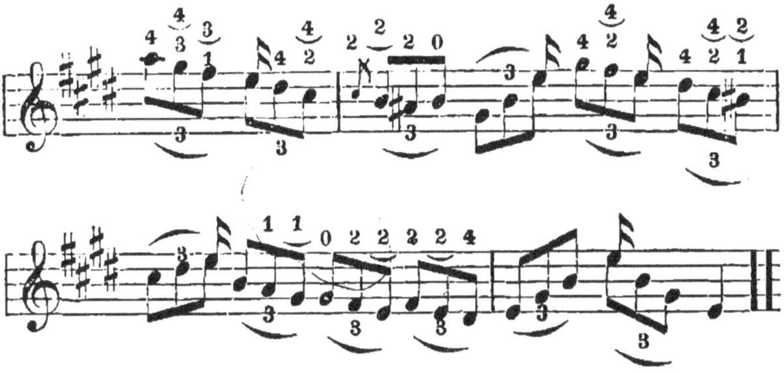

THE IVY WALTZ.

By W. H. RICHARDSON.

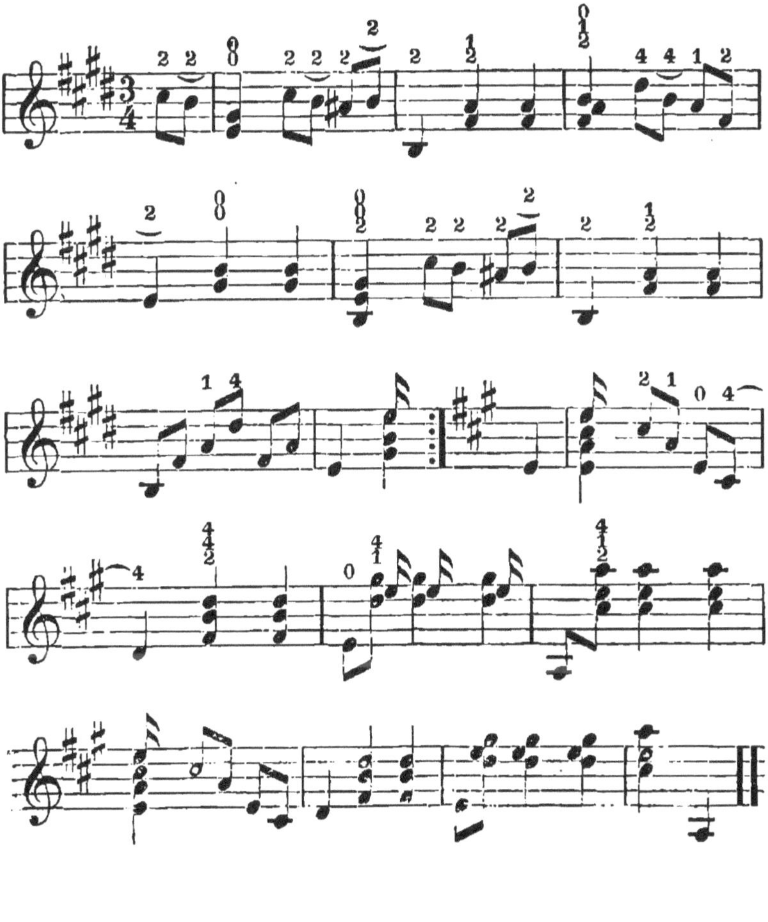

THE CREAM-COLORED HORSE.

Prelude.   As sung by HARRY STANWOOD.

1. Oh! lis-ten to me, I've a sad tale of woe, A

heart-rend-ing sto - ry that you must all know, Of a

beau-ti - ful girl who had me for her beau: To

mar - ry we both did a - gree.   Our

vows were most solemn - ly plighted,   It

made me so hap - py, of course;   Like a

cabbage my hopes she then blighted   For a

THE BANJO,

man on a cream-colored horse. Oh! He

rode 'round the ring with the greatest of care, He

shot thro' the hoop like a bul-let thro' cheese, He'd

stand on his head, while his toe he would seize, And

flip flap all o - ver the ring.

2.

I took 'Liza Jane to the circus, one night,
To witness this artist equestrian's flight,
She applauded so loud they all thought she was tight,
   Oh, goodness! how jealous I got.
Says I, " 'Liza Jane, now be quiet!"
   Says she, " Mister, you're not my boss,"
When she yelled for a cent's worth of pea-nuts
   For this man on the cream-colored horse.—*Cho.*

3.

He came out again with a flap and a whirl;
When he came right side up, he then winked at my girl;
I had a great notion my cane for to twirl
   At this man in his spangles and tights.
She threw him a kiss back so quickly,
   For my feelings she had no respect;
Now as he rode 'round in the circle,
   I wished that he might break his neck.—*Cho.*

4.

Now when we went home, we'd a terrible row,
I called her false-hearted, she'd broken her vow;
Says she, " Quit my sight, I'm done with you now,
   I'm engaged to the star of the ring.
I'll be called on the bills Senorita,
   We'll travel together, of course;
I'll do a flip flap on his eyebrow,
   As he rides on his cream-colored horse."—*Cho.*

SPANISH WALTZ.

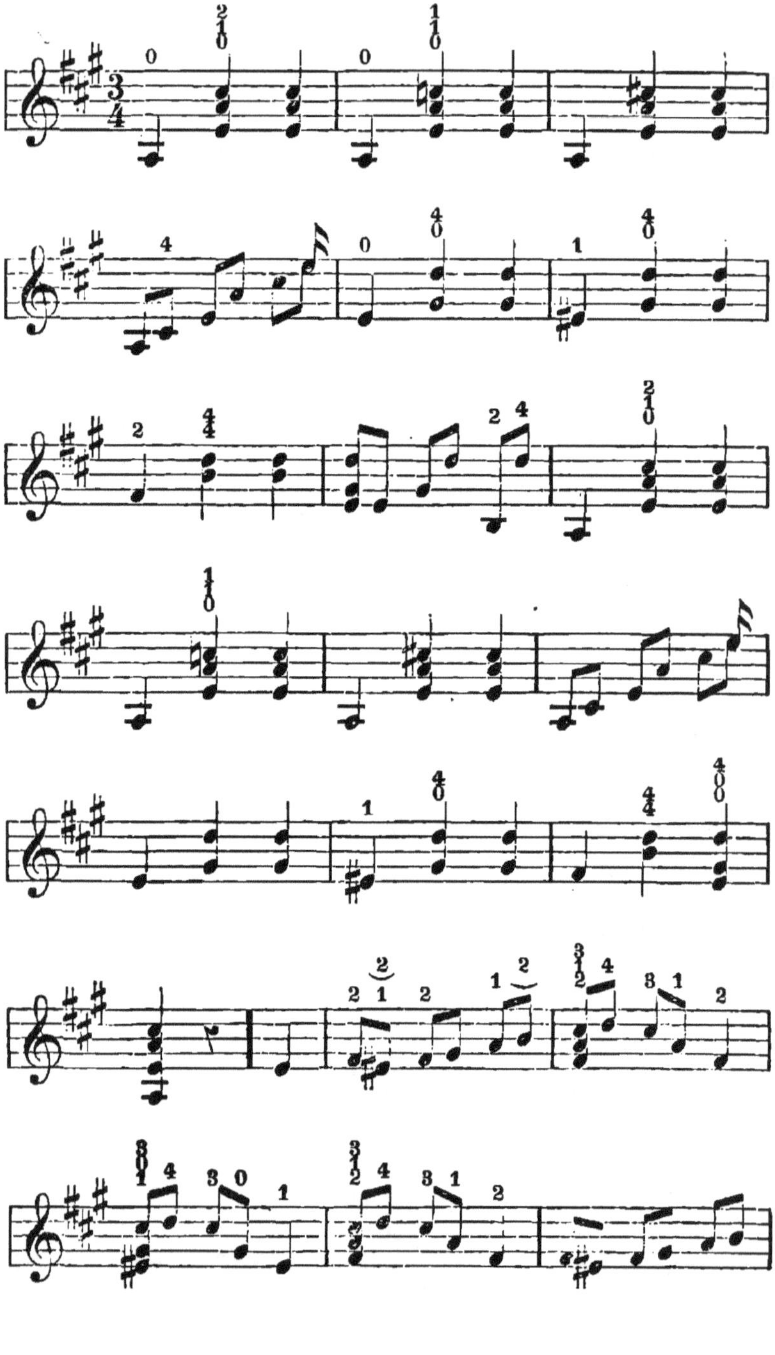

THE GRACE POLKA.

FINE.

CHECKERS AND CHESS.

Spayth's American Draught Player; or, The Theory and Practice of the Scientific Game of Checkers. Simplified and Illustrated with Practical Diagrams. Containing upwards of 1,700 Games and Positions. By Henry Spayth. Sixth edition, with over three hundred Corrections and Improvements. Containing: The Standard Laws of the Game—Full instructions—Draught Board Numbered—Names of the Games, and how formed—The "Theory of the Move and its Changes" practically explained and illustrated with Diagrams—Playing Tables for Draught Clubs—New Systems of numbering the Board—Prefixing signs to the Variations—List of Draught Treatises and Publications chronologically arranged. Bound in cloth, gilt side and back...$3.00

Spayth's Game of Draughts. By Henry Spayth. This book is designed as a supplement to the author's first work, "The American Draught Player"; but it is complete in itself. It contains lucid instructions for beginners, laws of the game, diagrams, the score of 364 games, together with 34 novel, instructive and ingenious "critical positions." Cloth, gilt back and side..$1.50

Spayth's Draughts or Checkers for Beginners. This treatise was written by Henry Spayth, the celebrated player, and is by far the most complete and instructive elementary work on Draughts ever published. It is profusely illustrated with diagrams of ingenious stratagems, curious positions and perplexing problems, and contains a great variety of interesting and instructive Games, progressively arranged and clearly explained with notes, so that the learner may easily comprehend them. With the aid of this Manual a beginner may soon become a proficient in the game. Cloth, gilt side...75 cts.

Scattergood's Game of Draughts, or Checkers, Simplified and Explained. With practical Diagrams and Illustrations, together with a Checker-Board, numbered and printed in red. Containing the Eighteen Standard Games, with over 200 of the best variations, selected from various authors, with some never before published. By D. Scattergood. Bound in cloth, with flexible covers...................................50 cts.

Marache's Manual of Chess. Containing a description of the Board and Pieces, Chess Notation, Technical Terms, with diagrams illustrating them, Laws of the Game, Relative Value of Pieces. Preliminary Games for Beginners, Fifty Openings of Games, giving all the latest discoveries of Modern Masters, with the best games and copious notes. Twenty Endings of Games, showing easiest ways of effecting Checkmate, Thirty-six ingenious Diagram Problems, and sixteen curious Chess Stratagems, being one of the best Books for Beginners ever published. By N. Marache. Bound in boards, cloth back...50 cts. Bound in cloth, gilt side..75 cts.

DICK & FITZGERALD, Publishers,

Box 2975.   NEW YORK.

DIALOGUE BOOKS.

The Dialogues contained in these books are all entirely original; some of them being arranged for one sex only, and others for both sexes combined. They develop in a marked degree the eccentricities and peculiarities of the various characters which are represented in them; and are specially adapted for School Exhibitions and other celebrations, which mainly depend upon the efforts of the young folks.

McBride's Comic Dialogues. A collection of twenty-three Original Humorous Dialogues, especially designed for the display of Amateur dramatic talent, and introducing a variety of sentimental, sprightly, comic and genuine Yankee characters, and other ingeniously developed eccentricities. By H. Elliott McBride. 180 pages, illuminated paper covers..30 cts. Bound in boards...50 cts.

McBride's All Kinds of Dialogues. A collection of twenty-five Original, Humorous and Domestic Dialogues, introducing Yankee, Irish, Dutch and other characters. Excellently adapted for Amateur Performances. 180 pages, illuminated paper covers...................30 cts. Bound in boards...50 cts.

Holmes' Very Little Dialogues for Very Little Folks. Containing forty-seven New and Original Dialogues, with short and easy parts, almost entirely in words of one syllable, suited to the capacity and comprehension of very young children. Paper covers.......................30 cts. Bound in boards, cloth back...50 cts.

Frost's Dialogues for Young Folks. A collection of thirty-six Original, Moral and Humorous Dialogues. Adapted for boys and girls between the ages of ten and fourteen years. By S. A. Frost. 176 pages, paper covers...30 cts. Bound in boards..50 cts.

Frost's New Book of Dialogues. Containing twenty-nine entirely New and Original Humorous Dialogues for boys and girls between the ages of twelve and fifteen years. 180 pages, paper covers..........30 cts. Bound in boards, cloth back...50 cts.

Frost's Humorous and Exhibition Dialogues. This is a collection of twenty-five Sprightly Original Dialogues, in Prose and Verse, intended to be spoken at School Exhibitions. 178 pages, paper covers.30 cts. Bound in boards...50 cts.

WE WILL SEND A CATALOGUE free to any address, containing a list of all the Dialogues in each of the above books, together with the number of boys and girls required to perform them.

DICK & FITZGERALD, Publishers,

Box 2975.   NEW YORK.

AMATEUR THEATRICALS.

All the plays in the following excellent books are especially designed for Amateur performance. The majority of them are in one act and one scene, and may be represented in any moderate-sized parlor, without much preparation of costume or scenery.

Burton's Amateur Actor. A complete guide to Private Theatricals; giving plain directions for arranging, decorating and lighting the Stage; with rules and suggestions for mounting, rehearsing and performing all kinds of Plays, Parlor Pantomimes and Shadow Pantomimes. Illustrated with numerous engravings, and including a selection of original Plays, with Prologues, Epilogues, etc. 16mo, illuminated paper cover.....30 cts.
Bound in boards, with cloth back...................................50 cts.

Parlor Theatricals; or, Winter Evenings' Entertainment Containing Acting Proverbs, Dramatic Charades, Drawing-Room Pantomimes, a Musical Burlesque and an amusing Farce, with instructions for Amateurs. Illustrated with engravings. Paper covers...........30 cts.
Bound in boards, cloth back....... .. ..50 cts.

Howard's Book of Drawing-Room Theatricals. A collection of twelve short and amusing plays. Some of the plays are adapted for performers of one sex only. 186 pages, paper covers...............30 cts.
Bound in boards, with cloth back..................................50 cts.

Hudson's Private Theatricals. A collection of fourteen humorous plays. Four of these plays are adapted for performance by males only, and three are for females. 180 pages, paper covers.................30 cts.
Bound in boards, with cloth back..................................50 cts.

Nugent's Burlesque and Musical Acting Charades. Containing ten Charades, all in different styles, two of which are easy and effective Comic Parlor Operas, with Music and Piano-forte Accompaniments. 176 pages, paper covers...30 cts.
Bound in boards, cloth back................:....................50 cts.

Frost's Dramatic Proverbs and Charades. Containing eleven Proverbs and fifteen Charades, some of which are for Dramatic Performance, and others arranged for Tableaux Vivants. 176 pages, paper covers.30 cts.
Bound in boards, with cloth back............. ....50 cts.

Frost's Parlor Acting Charades. These twelve excellent and original Charades are arranged as short parlor Comedies and Farces, full of brilliant repartee and amusing situations. 182 pages, paper covers..30 cts.
Illuminated boards... ....50 cts.

Frost's Book of Tableaux and Shadow Pantomimes. A collection of Tableaux Vivants and Shadow Pantomimes, with stage instructions for Costuming, Grouping, etc. 180 pages, paper covers..30 cts.
Bound in boards, with cloth back..................................50 cts.

Frost's Amateur Theatricals. A collection of eight original plays; all short, amusing and new. 180 pages, paper covers......30 cts.
Bound in boards, with cloth back..................................50 cts.

WE WILL SEND A CATALOGUE containing a complete list of all the pieces in each of the above books, together with the number of male and female characters in each play, to any person who will send us their address. Send for one.

DICK & FITZGERALD, Publishers,
Box 2975. NEW YORK.

Dick's Original Album Verses and Acrostics.

Containing Original Verses

For Autograph Albums;	*For Album Dedications;*
To Accompany Bouquets;	*To Accompany Philopena Forfeits;*
For Birthday Anniversaries;	*For Congratulation;*
For Wooden, Tin, Crystal, Silver and	*For Valentines in General, and all*
Golden Weddings;	*Trades and Professions.*

It contains also Two Hundred and Eighteen Original Acrostic Verses, the initial letters of each verse forming a different Lady's Christian name, the meaning and derivation of the name being appended to each. The primary object of this book is to furnish entirely fresh and unhacknoyed matter for all who may be called upon to fill and adorn a page in a Lady's Album; but it contains also new and appropriate verses to suit Birthday, Wedding, and all other Anniversaries and Occasions to which verses of Compliment or Congratulation are applicable. Paper covers. Price..50 cts.
Bound in full cloth.. " ..75 cts.

The Debater, Chairman's Assistant, and

Rules of Order. A manual for Instruction and Reference in all matters pertaining to the Management of Public Meetings according to Parliamentary usages. It comprises :

How to Form and Conduct all kinds of Associations and Clubs;	*Rules of Order, and Order of Business, with Mode of Procedure in all Cases.*
How to Organize and Arrange Public Meetings, Celebrations, Dinners, Picnics and Conventions;	*How to draft Resolutions and other Written Business;*
Forms for Constitutions of Lyceums or Institutes, Literary and other Societies;	*A Model Debate, introducing the greatest possible variety of points of order, with correct Decisions by the Chairman;*
The Powers and Duties of Officers, with Forms for Treasurers', Secretaries', and other Official Reports;	*The Rules of Order, in Tabular Form, for instant reference in all Cases of Doubt that may arise, enabling a Chairman to decide on all points at a glance.*
The Formation and Duties of Committees;	

The Work is divided into different Sections, for the purpose of Consecutive Instruction as well as Ready Reference, and includes all Decisions and Rulings up to the present day. Paper covers......................30 cts.
Bound in boards, cloth back....................................50 cts.

Dick's Ethiopian Scenes, Variety Sketches

and Stump Speeches. Containing End-Men's Jokes,

Negro Interludes and Farces;	*Dialect Sketches and Eccentricities;*
Fresh Dialogues for Interlocutor and Banjo;	*Dialogues and Repartee for Interlocutor and Bones;*
New Stump Speeches;	*Quaint Burlesque Sermons;*
Humorous Lectures;	*Jokes, Quips and Gags.*

It includes a number of Amusing Scenes and Negro Acts, and is full of the side-splitting vagaries of the best Minstrel Troupes in existence, besides a number of Original Recitations and Sketches in the Negro Dialect. 178 pages, paper covers..30 cts.
Bound in boards, cloth back......................50 cts.

Dick's Dutch, French and Yankee Dialect

Recitations. An unsurpassed Collection of Droll Dutch Blunders, Frenchmen's Funny Mistakes, and Ludicrous and Extravagant Yankee Yarns, each Recitation being in its own peculiar dialect. To those who make Dialect Recitations a speciality, this Collection will be of particular service, as it contains all the best pieces that are incidentally scattered through a large number of volumes of " Recitations and Readings," besides several new and excellent sketches never before published.

170 pages, paper cover.............................30 cts.
Bound in boards, cloth back.....................50 cts.

Dick's Irish Dialect Recitations. A carefully

compiled Collection of Rare Irish Stories, Comic, Poetical and Prose Recitations, Humorous Letters and Funny Recitals, all told with the irresistible Humor of the Irish Dialect. This Collection contains, in addition to new and original pieces, all the very best Recitations in the Irish Dialect that can be gathered from a whole library of " Recitation" books. It is full of the sparkling witticisms and queer conceits of the wittiest nation on earth; and, apart from its special object, it furnishes a fund of the most entertaining matter for perusal in leisure moments.

170 pages, paper cover.............................30 cts.
Bound in boards, cloth back.....................50 cts.

Worcester's Letter-Writer and Book of Busi-

ness Forms for Ladies and Gentlemen. Containing Accurate Directions for Conducting Epistolary Correspondence, with 270 Specimen Letters, adapted to every Age and Situation in Life, and to Business Pursuits in General; with an Appendix comprising Forms for Wills, Petitions, Bills, Receipts, Drafts, Bills of Exchange, Promissory Notes, Executors' and Administrators' Accounts, etc., etc. This work is divided into two parts, the portion applicable to Ladies being kept distinct from the rest of the book, in order to provide better facilities for ready reference. The Orthography of the entire work is based on Worcester's method, which is coming more and more into general use, from the fact that it presents less ambiguity in spelling. 216 pages. Bound in boards, cloth back....**50 cts.**

GOOD BOOKS

www.ingramcontent.com/pod-product-compliance
Lightning Source LLC
Chambersburg PA
CBHW031442280326
41927CB00038B/1543